Unlocking

Mary-Jane Newton

UNLOCKING is Mary-Jane Newton's second book of verse. In this vibrant new collection, Newton evokes a life experienced in cycles, characterized by peaks and troughs, fecundity and sterility, growth and retrenchment, optimism and despair. And punctuating these cycles, an infinite array of new beginnings, or openings, or "un-lockings". The poems in this collection insist that unlocking concerns more than simply change and transition. It involves too the stretching of the mind and body, the catharsis of deep emotion, and the rethinking of ideas and habits.

MARY-JANE NEWTON was born in India and grew up in Germany. Her first collection of poetry, *Of Symbols Misused* (2011), was also published by Proverse Hong Kong, and her work has appeared in numerous literary journals and anthologies internationally. She is Publishing Manager at Macmillan Publishers China and currently lives in Hong Kong with her husband and daughter.

Unlocking

Mary-Jane Newton

Proverse Hong Kong

Unlocking
by May-Jane Newton.
1st published in Hong Kong by Proverse Hong Kong, March 2014.
Copyright © Proverse Hong Kong, March 2014.
ISBN 978-988-8227-20-4

Distribution (Hong Kong and worldwide):
The Chinese University Press, The Chinese University of Hong Kong,
Shatin, New Territories, Hong Kong SAR.
E-mail: cup-bus@cuhk.edu.hk Web site: www.chineseupress.com
Tel: [INT+852] 3943-9800; Fax: [INT+852] 2603-7355
Distribution (United Kingdom):
Christine Penney, Stratford-upon-Avon, Warwickshire CV37 6DN,
England.
Email: <chrisp@proversepublishing.com>
Distribution enquiries: Proverse Hong Kong, P.O. Box 259,
Tung Chung Post Office, Tung Chung, Lantau Island, NT,
Hong Kong SAR, China.
E-mail: proverse@netvigator.com Web site: www.proversepublishing.com

The right of Mary-Jane Newton to be identified as the author of this work
has been asserted by her
in accordance with the Copyright, Designs and Patents Act 1988.

Printed in Hong Kong by Artist Hong Kong Company, Unit D3, G/F,
Phase 3, Kwun Tong Industrial Centre, 448-458 Kwun Tong Road,
Kowloon, Hong Kong.
Cover design by Andrew Magee Design Ltd.
Page design by Proverse Hong Kong.

British Library Cataloguing in Publication Data.
A catalogue record for this book is available
from the British Library.

From Memory to Memory

It is my pleasure to introduce you to a magnificent book of poems by Mary-Jane Newton. This book is filled with chilling, rasping, absorbing poems that charm and delight in their audacity. Infused with strength, *Unlocking* feels as natural as the leaves changing in autumn and the warmth of the sun slowly fading into night. These poems are wild and beautiful.

Unlocking opens with the cunningly titled, 'Safeguarding', which is an opening connection to one of the many intentions investigated in this book. Being locked, secure, sheltered within a symphonic setting where the writer is fastened within her own stupor. She is asking the reader to steady her, balance her with simple words so that she may "survive the crescendo." The idea of being unguarded in our time is revolutionary. To not be in lockdown, but free in a world locked tight by our secure systems that guard international travel, communications and limit our perceived liberties. Here the author, the authority of this work, is asking the reader to "draw a steady tangent", and be willing to make resounding positive declarations, as if one is asked to build a visual bridge between the living and the unborn.

I know my place
and look no further.
　(From 'Safeguarding')

Shadows play across this story of non-being, in a time where silence and subtlety are the main attractions. The shapes resulting tell us about relation, about the shifts, disappearances, and returns that express evolution. How we share imagination, authenticity; and acceptance is informed by the transformations within the self.

Unlocking goes after this with exactness and an eye for those unassuming occasions that fall between the fractures. In that place, Newton introduces stark changes. From the mythic transitions of growth, to the unseen terrors hiding right above our heads, to the overwhelming numbers of our world, as a tribute to the enshrined relevance of the contemporary waiting to break as a single straw piled upon a million more that will eventually break the proverbial camel's back.

Seven million nobodies
for a nothing in this world,
we cry, cry, cry
for survival
from obscurity.
    (*From 'Pennies'*)

It is at this point a break happens in the text and in the arcing narrative. A break in the outlook of the poet occurs. An unlocking of the self emerges, unrestrained. Moving from memory to memory, Newton explores the state, or rather the states, we are in, with poems of remarkable power. Taking up the challenge of seeing the self from many angles of being, she turns them into engines of poetic energy. Relentless and pessimistic, these poems cut grooves into the key and unlock the bolt holding back the difference between the safe and the guarded. *Unlocking* explores the ethical dilemmas inherent in the act of creation. Discovering the dark underside of creativity with rigour and humor. Part phenomenology and part phrenology, these poems are "bent … in a question mark" along the silken hook of an apology, to find its "sliver of time."

    Newton's work is arduous, metamorphic, offering itself as a response to the philosophical questions it poses. How, in the end, do we create security from insecurity? She encourages connectivity that demands we survive if only to find reclamation.

Silent memories now, so far back;
it might as well be the beginning.
Memories I can't quite trust,
shifting like clouds, talking over one another,
like wet gravel glinting under the sun.
   (*From 'Unlocking'*)

These poems are deceptively simple. There is a grace written into these lines that I find particularly engaging. In their directness and utter honesty these poems are wrapped in a bow, as a newborn, given away as a present to the laundry lady by a drug-addicted father.

You gave me away at my most needy,
dense and silent like a bag of laundry.
And you, you had the nerve to hunger?
   (*From 'Addict'*)

Geoffrey Gatza
Buffalo, NY, USA
October 2013

A Note on *Unlocking*

The notion of unlocking is described by American writer Kurt Vonnegut Jnr in his collection of essays, *Palm Sunday: Bits of the Collage* (1981). Here Vonnegut suggests that the four neat categories of spring, summer, autumn and winter fail to take account of the phenomenon, familiar in the northern hemisphere at least, of a gradual descent into, and subsequent equally gradual ascent out of, full-blown winter—indeterminate periods that Vonnegut christens "locking" and "unlocking". After locking comes the barren, infertile time of winter; and after unlocking comes the new growth, renaissance, rising sap and, consequently, perennial optimism of spring.

I try now to recognise and celebrate unlocking, in all its forms, as the beginning of the climb towards hope and as the threshold of rebirth. May the poems in this collection both bear testament to and encourage in others this readiness to see out the winter, stretch one's legs and move on, with confidence, to pastures new.

Mary-Jane Newton
Hong Kong
October 2013

Table of Contents

V   Sheets of Slate
VI Still Bleeding
VII After the Contract

For Ella, and all others who sparkle

I can't understand why people are
frightened of new ideas.
I am frightened of the old ones.

John Milton Cage Jr
From Richard Kostelanetz (1988), *Conversing with Cage.*

I

Yes! and *Yes!*

Safeguarding

Larger the trombones,
proud and bald-headed
shrieking yellow suns.
An owlish horn.

Drums, tight-lipped,
raging with stunning rapidity,
hissing dragons.

I, frozen aural butterfly
struck, mid-flight, and against
my will pinned to a board
and held there, am in stupour.

Bows and strings, tenacious
like the scent of sundown.
A single harp's
livid cry.

But through
the skulls, the noise, the bluster
I can still hear them,
your words'
soft and simple
symphony.

You'll stop
my plunge, break
my nightfall,
draw a steady tangent.
Yes! and *Yes*!

Now
Lay your hand on my breast
so that I may survive
the crescendo.

You, Becoming

To my unborn daughter

With you, becoming,
I bend, an easy equator,
blow, a wind of blossoms.
—You pod of slight energy,
growing in centrifugal force!

An unfolding in the softest *ville*,
you move in the air above
and below and around me,
give birth to all colours.

You render nothing rounded,
but all radiant and edgy, fill
my days with divine
discontent and longing.

All are strangers, but the city
holds you in my hands of streets
and folds you in the creases
of my oldest rhythm.

With you, becoming, I travel
like the light, span the poles,
sway like warmed mercury.
You are my furthest star,
my rocket, my spaceman.

The unthinkable:
I gather all the threads,
lost and loose, and descend to
the bare bones of life,
see intimately into the insides of

things, which expose themselves,
pathetically, pitifully, and yet
cheering, in exhilarated swindle.
Layers of finery everywhere,

strong and simple. With you,
I leave them, penetrated,
empty cartridges of
machinegun ammunition
that pulsate and glitter
—a sky of stars.

Kodama[1]

They were days of theft, our days in the woods. Let's not
have it otherwise. Days and days of an enormous,
uncanny
darkness forever punctured by pale and bulbous eyes,
and twig-like legs with knotted muscles, scuttling. No
walls

could keep us protected, no hope could keep us from
being
peeled of our skins and left there, in the sullen open, prey
to all those gaping eyes and noises, scufflings and
hurryings
that made our heads turn and our bodies jitter. We were

looking for something we could not find nor remember
what
it looked like, when we spotted them, finally, on the
branches
in the eerie forest green; their luminous heads turning,
like
small, round clocks clicking and creaking in the twilight.

We dared not venture close, so as not to confess our
folly, but
the woods would brook no disclaimer, no counterclaim.
So we
stood, watching closely yet from afar, and they followed
us
into our dreams. Until, one day, the helter-skelter ceased,
and

there were no more heads or green things to be found.

We
searched as we were left in wonder and surprise, for
something
we could not look for nor knew that we remembered.
And the
woods remained tall and silent, and groaned in their
lethargy

and dolour. The moss, the bracken endured the lack; the
woodland floor cradled the last of the light footprints.
We think
of them fondly now, our days of theft, and the soft sap
that ran
down the pines and gathered in viscid drops on dark
brown bark.

Scales

For Toby

Your rawness to break me open
like a ripe fruit; your wet flesh to
break me in, bring me thunder,
flush my cheeks;

your age to shape our lines of gold,
ceaseless rings of Saturn; your
tongue to draw the crimson
seeds of pomegranates;

your words to lie and speak
the deepest truth; your exuberance
to set me free, to join my broken
spine of pearl;

your thought to lash my blood,
my ice, my frenzy; your hands
to quench my thirst; your black
to douse my white.

Your salt to lick my wounds;
our communion to stir the devils,
crack the barrier of sound.
Our palms to meet,

our weights to shift
the scales of time and justice.

Apology

If I forgot that I have swallowed you, silken hook,
forgive me.
Forgive me, if I yielded to cunning: to your silver thread
and
diamond sinker—if I gorged on them, cleft the roof of
my
mouth, scraped the inside of my throat, slit my thought,
and

smiled in my contentment. Silken hook, forgive me, if I
have
made you equal to my chief joy, bent my body in a
question mark
to match your rolling guise, forged my words to suit your
integrity.
Silken hook, I know you're but a sliver of time.

We were never meant to bring one another to maturity.
Now that my bones are
parched by rapid age, I plead forgive me—forgive me,
for my

willful ignorance. Stiff-necked, I believed I carried
within me
the All, believed I wandered as the essence in the world.
I could
not resist your beauty. I am gagging now. Ret-ret-
retching on
you, silken hook, inducing the moment I can take a deep
breath.

Wisdom

A sob, unerringly,
gathering, gathering, gathering
somewhere low down inside
to leap up to the surface in
passionate escape. There was no
delaying longer; it refused
to be beaten.

So up and up
it forced its way to the air and then
another and others, thick and fast
until she gave up the struggle and
cried freely, helplessly and openly,
shook, stretched, muscles mere water.

She bowed her head, but still,
as she looked, she lived, and still,
as she lived, she wondered about
the absence of tears.

She looked up
to the sky;
it was a sky golden and
always dancing, shimmering,
softly talking, or swaying strongly
with the passing wind and
recovering itself with a toss
and merry laugh.

Now I Wish to Wait

When I was young,
I toyed with others' hearts
the way new kittens play
with balls of wool, the way
the wind dallies in a chime.

I'm slower now,
but, yes, more graceful, and
I know it is not me
they are talking about.

I remember well,
my outrage sought to take
the moorings from the ground,
the heather from the hill.
I could have taken the willow
from the root,
the limpet from the crag,
the eagle from its young.

Age has taught me
there is no need to rush,
has taught me
I can afford to be generous,
and now I wish to wait.

I used to catch the wind
in caves of ice,
and dreamt of red mountains
and landscapes of rock,
and hollows filled
with water and fading light,

and rain drifting as veils
over the peaks and beyond,
and, in the distances, there was
a warm gleam on the sea.

But, you know,
there is something to be said for
the mild weather and the thought
that precedes one's actions.

When I was young,
I felt the night wind on my face,
and joy and anguish in my heart.
I climbed the grit stone peaks,
and came down
in blazing sparks of fire.

Now, the moon rises
above the quiet lakes
and there's no call for praise—
I know my place
and look no further.

II

Soft Brutality

Panama City, 1933

Structures of the airport, newly-built, are draped with sweet and
sickly heat that stands up silently, old and hot against the ceiling.

Three dusty, stubborn fans knead the viscous air;
withhold themselves
from the waiting man, stout and wheezy, pressed into a
plastic airport chair.

A languid, weary creature of large yet feeble
composition; expanded,
enormous, with a big, pale head and swollen legs, he sits
and sweats

in swathes of raw heat. Somewhere: the buzzing of a fly.
Its struggle is distant, small and unimportant. It does not
reach him.

His damp linen suit feels alien to his amorphous thighs.
Undignified, his body—
a soft brutality—spills into the neighbouring seat like
Dali's

clock. The fly's oscillating buzz now finds its way into
his consciousness:
a useless fussing of a tiny, energetic organism. He cannot
see it. Under his

enormous brows, his eyes blink pathetically. His vast
indolence finds

it difficult to tolerate any reminder of agility, sedulity, or
lightness. He breaks out

in another noxious sweat, lifts his hat and dabs his
forehead with a
yellowed handkerchief. His hair, wet and salty, adorns
his forehead like

an array of swamp algae. He inhales flatly, puffs his
cheeks. A drop of sweat
plummets from the ridge above his brow and shatters on
the tile

beneath his leather shoe. The fly grows vague. Its drone,
tinier now,
is carried off into the halls above, cavernous and wide
and indistinct.

Poem No. 165

Wants to remain unknown, unwritten. Wants to cry
hoarsely that this
is not the fate it has deserved;

would rather inject its host with poison
and turn pale and waxen, than assume shape, become
"meaningful", be forced
into a pattern strange and peregrine;

would rather age and rot an unborn
virgin, be forgotten like an age-old monument;

would rather drown in other
stories, tales and poems, or be hanged with rattling
emotion;

would rather
seek a private battle with its host, than be told, captured
with words. Being
captured with words means to search for the cross on the
map, and searching for
the cross on the map means to take the first step on a
course inevitable. Broken,
blackened stumps of feet would scratch the paper, and a
thumping sound
would pump from every cranny, every letter. Marauding
feet would rush.
The journey would unfold in a thousand winding
courses. In every turn and
every syllable, change would brood like the dark twin of
death.

Would rather
crumble into fragments, black and ominous and blurred
by memory, rather shift
into a dream of greed and violence, or grow into a
different being altogether;

wants to pivot, tighten, growl in suicidal rage: "Go on
then, stunt, distort and warp
me with your useless, little language!"

Wants to remain a secret, wants to remain
true.

Metamorphosis

Und als ich aufsah, war sie nimmer da.
(Bertold Brecht—Erinnerung an Marie A.)[2]

I looked up and saw a great white bird of prey,
bulky, yet handsome, travelling low and langorous
in a marbled sky studded with shapes my mind could not
assemble. There was no denying it, it was a bird

with a wing prolonged and fibrous, a sharp head and
a pale, curved beak perched on a body high and
bulging. But as I looked, still occupied with the
perception of its gestalt, there, under my very eyes, it
began

to crumble, to disintegrate here, develop there,
shift and twist and calibrate; began to divide its wing
in four, erect a quadruplet of legs, askew and disparate,
began to fuse the beak and head to one great muzzle.

Then, for a moment, the monstrosity paused. But before
long,
one side of its body thinned into a neck, knitted and
strong,
and its back morphed into that of a horse. But there it
did not stop. Leaking wisps of white into the sky—parts

of its head, neck, and mane—it began to abandon its
legs. I felt a sense of quiet panic and strained in the
adjustment of my vision. But before I knew it, I could
no longer bear the terror. I cast my glance to trees
nearby.

Death of a Cat³

The cat is out of the bag

Should I skin it?
Or harpoon it? The death blow!
Easy, push back its little head,
sever its carotids,
both of them ... *fssss!*

(Guillotine in reverse.)
Or shoot it perhaps?
Machine gunners galore,
rat-rat-rat-rat!
Like grinding coffee by hand.

Bomb it to pieces perchance?
Flutter and shrapnel ... *boom!*
Bursting, flying fragments.
Or burn it? Roasted meat,
clots of soot, blood and hair.

Stone it? Disembowel it?
Flushed, bubbling depths ...
gurgle! Or choke it?
Or drown it?
In formaldehyde?

No more murmuring maybes
for you, buddy fluffball!
No more sitting, thousand-yard stare,
like a soft little raspberry,
in sickening superiority!

That's it, you're a goner,
goody-two-shoes! No more
bristling mustaches,
perking your tail! Where are
my crutches, my dentures?

The chase is on ...

Xue-Li[4]

comes as if it was
today, this morning;

Koi[5]-tailed eyes
and long, black hair,
fool's gold in a

summer's
lake.

Xue-li ...water runs
(sun splashes)
on her back, pearls,
sighs for hunger,
licks her breast.

But sadly dumb as bone;
a sorry little simpleton,
bobbing head on a stake,
grunting gastric tubes,
bla-bla-blabbering.
If only we could

tell by Koi-tailed
eyes the depth

of our
intellects ...

Childhood

It's an ugly truth:
we spend our childhoods
as if they were inexhaustible.

Milojka ran after that frantic chicken in her
shoes made from old tyres and I tucked
into my maize bread watching her.

Those fish we caught on summer days,
the tails we grabbed to shatter
their heads and throw them back
into the beck, and how they drifted
down the stream, eyes fixed and rigid,
with their sides to the sunlight,
silver twinkling.

As a child, I always found the right
words. But now I cramp and jitter,
and nurse those doubts sawing up the world.

And grandma, *Baba*,[6] with her
blue-veined, arthritis-bitten fingers,
how she rubbed me down in the
bathtub and sleeked my hair
with butter; how she fed me whole
cloves of garlic, and sang, and sang,
and sang more,
and the hissing black-and-white TV.

The turtle shell we hammered down on,
never thinking that a stone could gather such
momentum,
could melt the blackest *almost*.

Pennies

Seven million
wriggling tiny agonies
behind whose smiles
lies the trembling
of the lost.

I, as all the others,
clutch my past;
am like the outside:
too big,
too *everywhere.*

Seven million nobodies
for a nothing in this world,
we cry, cry, cry
for survival
from obscurity.

Nauseated looks
on bloated faces:
seven million
dead skins that form
a sloughing flatness:

regimented plant life,
hanging and swelling
with the
taste of pennies
in our mouths.

The Camel's Back

You;
your beautiful neck.

I'm no longer stoic
about
something
enormous.

I think:
I should have
brought
an axe.

The Stone-numberer

Heavy and changeless
were his eyes,
as if from a cage.
And on, to the quarry!

Strange as it may seem,
horror loses
its power to horrify
when repeated all too often.

III

Taste Another Drop

Enter and Name

Enter this poem through the prison door,
the madhouse door, the brothel door.
And once you've entered, study the others:
the golden and green doors, these that rotate
and those that slide open.
The doors as small as keyholes, the padded ones
and the ones studded with nails.
The ones that have been cut from paper
and the ones that unbutton like an old suit.
The ones that gape like the entrances to caves,
and these others as thick as treasure chests.
This one that looks like a sweet child's mouth
and this one here that opens like a drawbridge.
The ones that are made of gingerbread, and the ones
that wind themselves like the houses of snails.
The doors that lurk like trap doors
and the doors that you need to forget to enter.

And then, name this poem.
Name it by its right name,
which will give it being and reality.
The wrong name will make it unreal.
That's what lies do.

Wintering

An epilogue of streets:
I feel the dry and steady drumming
of a great white heart unknown.
Frantic and still at once.
A great momentum grips me.

Winter drives its knives
as hardened flakes into my chest.
A gust of wind, silent and
chamomile-scented,
glazes my eyes, mats my greying hair with frost.
I've eaten of an ancient fear.
Forgive me for my patience.
I've loved you long and dearly.

Below: a bitter snow's gnashing teeth.
Above: a single star freezes.
And I walk fast, however wintering.

How to be Victorious

And fashion them, my brown bones,
into something sharp and elegant
with which to pierce my flesh.

And the poison ivy, and my sickly heart,
a carnival freak, a rattling toy,
and the last letter, "A".

And the cankerous blossoms of a
tremendous fog, *Istigkeit*,[7]
undoing everything.

And crush it, the sponge, and
taste another drop.

Morning After

I had made love to him.
It felt like being sapped
and lulled by sunburn.

I felt *seen*. Then, I left.
We broke like sheets
of ice, drifted apart like

two comic strip panels
disjoined by
a jagged line.

No more lace.
No more
platitudes.

And nothing lost,
but everything
transformed.

That is to Say

That is to say,
the searching eyes,
the word unheard,
or the blues,
that bastard
that pounces on you
whenever you least expect it.

Honey and Ashes

Now I want you only more.
I need to go out; I've just come back in.
It is the season of Earth dying,
of something in-between.

Skin tingles.
And what one knows in one's cheating heart,
and what one says, are two different things.

The word.
This universal solvent, freezedries, disintegrates
with an acrid smell of paralysis.

Clawed from the air, mid-flight,
as if I was a gift, you dropped me,
mound of mangled flesh and quill,
on the doorstep of fate.

You *created* me.
Now you slip from my hands.

I know. I know this:
love's a crisis of the soul and
the most exquisite thing is a sting to the heart.

Bite my knuckles, hands jerk open,
and among those thousand
kisses day in, day out, this one is the last,
your wet cheek the taste of bitter walnuts.

The Red of My Heart

In all Mesopotamia
they speak of me, Sargon,[8]
"The Soldier of Soldiers," they say.
My armour, my skin
is my silent servant:
this is the red of my heart.

In paradise the ages are spent,
poured out like guttered candles.
We drink to get drunk.
We sour our blood.
We trade in truths that are not ours.
My thoughts so rarely now
rise above these sagging shoulders.
This is the red of my heart.

You said, "goodbye" or "welcome"
(I can't remember which),
and you insisted, "Sargon's sword
is the boldest and quickest."
But who are you now?
Who are the passers-by
we call our friends?
Blunt my dagger
that has seen so many backs.
I no longer fight.
I've grown old,
and this is the red of my heart.

We sleep, we eat,
we do as puppets do.
We smile our wooden smiles and nod.
We cloak our inner savage child
in the frail clothes of maturity.
We pay with coins of
little value for the deaths
our teachers die.

Between two lungs
this breath was born,
between the halves of a single heart
this tragic love.
It is the red of my heart, you see,
the red of our hearts we butcher.

IV

Next Manhole

Another Aging

The last grain of sand—held between
these walls and bound by them, motionless,
locked by molecules, particle on particle
finally displacing—comes crushing down,
a thunderous roar, a burning train wreck
still on its rails, crashing through and through
and through me, blasting its course;
regret for a forgotten deed,
the last comet in your twinkling eyes,
love's tender death:
time has made a meal of you.

The First Coat of The Day

And as the sun set, the enormous
grinder of lenses, he cramped
in pain, tore asunder, and
produced an offspring of thick
honey and mist. Warm, pale, gentle
radiance, he set him adrift, then tilted
his sweet countenance into my chambers.

He held a zither in his hand,
a golden treasure. He learned me back
to childhood, stole my fright, and
crawled into my stronghold, my refuge,
took root and drank—voraciously—
my drying blood. Smiling, he came close,
the Lord of Light and Ivory, and gouged

his zither in my chest. No pain to
sting, burn, corrode. But breathing suddenly
seemed arduous. Smiling velvetly,
he left me behind as I was, penetrated
and shivering, and silver glinting stardust
floated in the air. He left in shimmering
light. The wound healed.

My mornings now, when I awake, are
filled with sweet side-string play;
sky-blue and damp, this is the first coat of the
day around me. Only sometimes, when seated,
can I feel the string ends' gentle prompting.

Sardines

The metal lid
breaks up,
grinds,
echoes.
Never we waver: this is our time,
comrades! *Now!* Stand *still!*
(As if we had a choice.)

Addict

To my father, who in a drug craze gave me,
a few-weeks-old infant, to the laundry lady
as a present

Goa, 1983.

Eyes not quite in register,
ashen and powdery,
too loud, too proud, too *gone*,
never a good audience for silence.

Yet you believed yourself in touch
with the far side of yourself,
as if witnessing something essential,
something brand new and profound,
a piece of the world so startling,
there was not yet a name for it.

Meanwhile, you were a lot like
yesterday. A lot like never.
To know that you gave me away!
In a box with red ribbons!

All you cared about was to
feel it ooze up over your body,
hollow your lungs, your heart
ricocheting in your ribcage.
You disappeared inside yourself,
grey and brittle, wet and swirling,
without sound or centre, like oil.

You gave me away at my most needy,
dense and silent like a bag of laundry.
And you, you had the nerve to hunger?

In all those years
you never so much as felt
your tongue against the truth.
So now feel the dumb, bitter soil ...
not quite as snug in your mouth
as an apology.

Life

A blossom
that nature has chanced on this tree
and the wind
has caressed just a touch too much,

I am ready
to plunge myself into the grit below,
land at my softest,
be crushed by rain stained shoes

or held briefly by rushing trouser legs,
or be swept away
amongst dusty cigarette butts
into the next manhole,

to accept it all, to journey.

With All Due Respect

You don't know a poem.

Not until you've seen it coming
morpheme by morpheme,
until it's wrapped its syntax around you and
wrung you out like a tired cloth, stabbed you
in the back, relished your death rattle,
until it's sent you kisses
and nightmares all day long.

Tock tock, let me in
I'm only a little vowel
I won't do any harm

You don't know a poem, old man.
You may be letting in rage, or worse still,
fate. You don't know a poem,
you don't know life.
That's the way it is, old codger:
Thank you and *Goodbye*.

Life's not a children's party
or a picnic in the sun.
You don't know life
until you've lived it
in your muscles and with
the sad habits of the heart,
until you've hung in the wind,
zig-zagged with the truth,
lain prostrate in the heat,
pierced paler the blade in war.

Not until your final throes have given rise
to the whisper of the mouldering roots
that darken like a dream,
crueler and gentler in turns.

Danny Ringwald

It was in our cave, under the table,
where he first showed me his Bratwurst[9]
and we used the kindergarten's toy cutlery to
cut it and pretend to eat. And he used to
go around people's houses and hold toy sales,
and my mother used to say,
"this boy has an excellent sense of business".

Much later, the teacher told us he was run over,
no, not actually run *over*, but run *into*,
and that it happened because he crossed the street
without waiting for the green light.
Let it be a lesson to all of us.
Later that day, on the way home,
we saw the blood stains on the street and little
plastic pieces of his school bag.
And while we were waiting for the green light
to cross the street, a middle-aged sleazy man
remarked on my High German.

Danny turned up after a few months with greenish
stitches
on his upper lip that we eyeballed with great curiosity,
but I still beat him on the race track.
I think he moved away, or I moved away,
or we changed schools, in any case, he was carried off
together with so many others, frozen in large sheets of
ice,
on a slow, polar sloom of narrative.

V

Sheets of Slate

Parting Glass

Remember Miss Cullen, thin as a wisp, whose presence I
could barely make out,
the Maths teacher, somewhat resinous, like a frog's
tongue, who was rumoured to have some disease,
something wrong with her thyroid, that made her shrill
and talk too fast.

Like things in museums,
barely alive and yet
rippling with significance,
bringing forth the Now;
history repeats itself;
rewrites the present.

And there was Mrs Roberts, married to a Frenchman,
who would blather away twenty minutes of a lesson if
you got her going. Of onion soup (good for a cough or a
cold), or her son, who went to university in France. A
vain woman, with tight lips and dark brown nail polish,
and puffy hair and scent.

It's satisfying the sad fierce appetite
of memory and sentimentalism;
a chimera, turned stupid
with every telling and re-telling of
that same old story …

And Mr Wilson, the Ethics teacher, who really was a
Professor, who could talk and who held forth in a way
that was not without interest, but who stank of alcohol
and old cigarettes so that—torn between wanting to learn
and the simple physics of air circulation—I sat in the

second row in Year 2, ducking and crouching to avoid
the worst of it.

The past: a slippery bed mat, a sly bastard
changing the DNA of your daily life
forever, an ageless night,
a fog of parting glass.

And the Physics teacher, whose name escapes me now,
who used to be a Formula 1 racer until he had an
accident that left his back immobile, and we used to
giggle when he couldn't pick up the chalk. Him and the
Biology teacher, who were rumoured to have a
relationship, and who must have known that I cheated
my way through every test and flushed the cheat sheet
down the toilet.

This was when we all held our breaths.
Everyone claims otherwise, but
the past is never over.

Daddy

You were a figure of shadow, an enigma,
not to be mentioned, so as not to stir mum's anger.
A single call you made from prison,
and your voice boomed through that chunky green
receiver, "Happy Birthday, I'll send your present later".
It was going to be a doll, I knew it, so I waited
but no parcel ever arrived. In sixteen years
you sent one postcard,
self-made, of cardboard,
with glued-on paper bars and a plastic daisy stuck
through.
How you must have suffered.
You sent it from a Sri Lankan prison
I much later found out.
A missed party prompted me to call you.
My Nirvana T-shirt, my finger, bitten nail, in a telephone
book. My uncle had told me you lived
in the neighbouring village.
I was fourteen or fifteen, or sixteen, I can't remember
now.
You picked me up, asked if I'd had brown sugar before. I
said "Of course; I'm young, but I've lived".
You took me to your house and gave me plenty to get
high on, plenty to adore you.
We met again and more often
and I saw the poppy plantation in your cellar,
full of radiators and fans, the floor covered with cables,
the trap door hidden beneath your washing rack. Today,
I'd have pity.
And you started to bring me my weekly fix,
enough for me and my friends, who thought I was so
cool with a daddy like that.

Inject it in your legs, that's where it goes unnoticed and
looks like a mere mosquito bite. You were a hero,
Daddy.
We were high when you pushed your hand between my
thighs and groped my small breasts.
"You've got your mum's figure," is what you said.
Your tongue was too wet, your arms like crowbars.
Oh and that tattoo with my date of birth under that palm
tree.
I couldn't even walk to the door anymore, my legs hurt
so much.
We met for whiskey when you told me it was your
birthday soon and that I would be all yours that night.
I knew you had bought yourself an electric mace
to keep unwanted junkies away.
I'd gone too far, I blame myself. I stopped answering the
phone.
In my dreams, you'd use that cow prod on me.
You were furious, "You're just like your mum, you
Yugoslavian scum," I hear it now.
Finally I had to tell. Mum and her boyfriend looked at
me with incredulous eyes. We wanted to sue
for all that money you never paid,
for all the drugs and the way you poisoned my youth.
But hey man, nothing you can do when there's no
money, when you've got a gambling problem too.
And the years swam on, and night on night stars moved
across the ocean. I felt sorry for you,
imagined your burden; to know what you had done to
me. Yes, I wanted you to apologize, make it up to me,
so I emailed you in the student hall.
You had a daughter now you said,
"But I am your daughter too," I answered.
You wrote loving mails and ones that were angry,
others that were gentle and more that were violent.

In your inefficient way, you stranded me,
like Robinson in that poem you once wrote.
Then, you said they wanted to take your daughter
away—just because of that small bruise on her head!
I knew she hadn't hit her head on the sink. I wrote my
letter to the police.
And then that phone call when I was at work: "I'm going
to die soon," you whined. I thought, "What a cheap
trick".
But then the last call came, a German voice,
whispering you had died in hospital.
A sick joke, I thought and called to make sure.
So there we are now, Daddy,
I've listened to your funeral song.
I ain't scared of dying and I don't really care.
I can swear there ain't no heaven but I pray there ain't
no hell.
It was your last hurrah, that silly, pathetic song.
I know you thought it mattered.
Now you loom like a fog in the distance. You are a
sandy path beneath my feet. You are sheets of slate
that grow and lie upon each other
and engender, finally, a precious stone.

Ella at Fourteen Months

The human spark—fire—
warm, gentle breath of
cinnamon and milk—closer to nature now
than ever again.

Fourteen months of animal needs,
cries, and saliva, of life as biosphere,
now no longer entirely moved
by a slow primordial spirit,
but ready to sign, shake her head,
knock the door,

call dogs and buses
baaa! and may have said mama this morning.
Not yet fully submerged
in the cacophony of thought and language—
upright posture, the wheel, the cog, the machine—
civilization, like us.

Remember how we called her Boogie
writhing and rumbling, just the other day,
like an antediluvian rockabilly, a segmented skeleton
revealed like a squirming ancient beast
uncovered by geologists, buried in my womb,
the rock of ages.

Now she is climbing on the sofa,
building Babel with her blocks,
risking her life soon on her tricycle.
Same age-old thoughts, hopes and fears
as the hominids who laid down the prints
of saber-toothed tigers:

a better, richer Earth, a place in which
she would delight to live.

She, like all of us,
arose from and belongs to the natural world.

Standstill

Don't
stand still
like the icicle.
Stand still
like the
hummingbird.[10]

Priorities

Be like
the sundial:

count
the light hours

and

fail to show up
for
the dark ones.

VI

Still Bleeding

The Job Interview, Experienced Under Conditions of Late Capitalism

I'm sorry, but we don't have the time
to run through your qualifications
in detail.

Just tell us,
and the Managing Director of Greater Asia here,
how much leverage you have,
how many, ahem, relationships you have forged
with the necessary gatekeepers,
whether you have rehearsed your Colgate smile,
and slicked your hair sufficiently.
You have parked your jalopy outside? Good.
And made sure the ring on your little finger
sits neatly?
Also good.

So, then, now,
to our final question:

What would you implement first
in your new role as a joke?

The Road Less Travelled

In response to Robert Frost

To the arms on my back,
between my shoulder blades;
to the push:

don't ask me. I am past thought.
My head has broken free of chaos.
Bushes now dictate my direction,
I take the famous path of least resistance.

Branches give way beneath my feet,
catch my limbs. Tough, crooked boughs,
long, pliant, wire-like shoots,
skeins of dead wood, lancets and splinters
and the dead growth underneath it all.

Malicious brambles, and branches that
swing higher at every jerk, roots sucking deep in the
mud.
The lanced thicket, the dull bracken, leaf-bearing
tentacles,
and no steel to tame the copse and slay the Gordian
Knots
gnawing at my ankles.

The bleak bark dust with the bitter taste to burn the
throat!
And the tall trees leaning towards
each other as if to share some dark, dark secret!

I'm hot and weary now, smarting from a hundred stings
and scratches.
No, not *travelling* anymore, I *tumble* down this path,
for what a road less travelled it is!

The Life in My Arms

For Ella Maude

"You be the robber, I the policeman,"
you will say, bending the rules
of our every game. Scraped knees forgotten,
you will embark on polar expeditions
as a fearless explorer
on Repulse Bay beach.
The spring in your step will match
the dappled sun on trees in your eyes;
your small laughter, your smile
you'll still give lightly to every stranger.
You'll count your glow-in-the-dark stars,
and fallen frangipani flowers,
and Peak tram rides,
and you'll never be home on time.
Who knows if you'll still be *you* then, and
I still *me*; you, the life in my arms,
my favourite Theseus' ship.[11]

B-15[12]

Your cries have ended now,
and you have scattered into the seismic sea.
You are a white giant, broken.

Like a newborn, you had
insinuated yourself between two lovers,
laid yourself on top of them—
an ill-fated Venn diagram.

There's a point to be made here:
things are never clear-cut,
and complexity always staggers
towards us from behind a corner.

So farewell, my baby,
sleep well in your bed of waves.

Still Bleeding

A war poem

For you,
I am still bleeding, dying in a world of wet.

Without the comfort of others,
without cease, red drops are falling, rolling
to a ground so cold, and mingling with
the sap of pines and the blending
scents of sopping wood and mushroom.

Why! It had never dawned on me
that when the two of us met, there were six people there.

And now it is too late to see them all
and know their nature. I am hit. I've fallen.
Crawled towards a cradle
too fragrant for my death. But I am tranquil,
for you are here

to surrender and catch the last of my breath
in the clear winter wind. And it is not true
what they say, and I have not again seen
the triumphs of life within the split second flit across my
eyes.

What I have seen, is you, my love,
and me, and what we truly were and who
we'll never be, and the blood that is
seeping into a harsh ground's fissures.
For you,
I am still bleeding.

All Yang

This incandescence is supposed to be the night?
How anyone can stand this vividness,
I don't know. Above all, it produces bad poetry,
—all emotion, no tranquility.

Have you seen?

It fills the distances between one dot and the next
with light, until all ellipses shine like little moons.
Like playing ducks and drakes with darkness:

a biography of two. (Or three?)

Let me try to say it, then, in a language that is not an
offence to language:

In my darkness, I owed nothing to his esteem,
and everything to his black-and-white art.

Arduous

is the
squirrel's
search
for food.

VII

After the Contract

Good Fortune

Then the pasture—
blades of grass
were smiling—

"Four-leafed clovers?"
And they shrugged
with the wind
and poured out
sympathy:
"Good fortune is
so rare a thing …"

Never attained,
the sixty-first minute
of the hour.
Always fading,
the last sad
star of a
pyrotechnic's display.

So then—
amid the honeysuckle
and wild plums
I plucked
a three-leafed fellow.
Fumbled its
limp body
into my pocket,
heavy with
hope.

After the Contract

Inspired by Don Paterson's work on the "poetic contract"

Let's be honest, who are we kidding here?
At least half of this poem came from you anyway.
It was your idea all along, to read this and that,
put your words into my mouth.

I don't mind your sweet talk, pat me on the back,
for all I care! In any case, I've lost control over my lines.
Storytelling has hijacked my poetry.
As if I could find a lyric *in a sentence!*

All I'm doing is giving you the space to sound,
to echo, to *over-attend*, to signify the hell out of this shit.
I'm a mover and shaker, and, you know it,
you want to be moved and shaken.

So let's stop all this silly pretense. Let's imagine
for a moment we've really got something to say.
Let's live to talk about it and spill ink
like nobody's business.

Appropriating

I've been meaning to make
these notes on paper, old-school,
like the person at the other end,
who'll decide whether or not to
print it in their journal,
naturally, over fifty and male,
but I never have any to hand,
so I've ended up using my smart phone again
and I've used the spelling
errors for effect.

The Smallest

Today, there are more ants,
and I keep stopping in my tracks.
You are dead, it's true,
truer things that can be true
and shifting prisms break.
Me, I often feel this way.

I itch!
These ants!
I fail to crush their poison bodies;
if only you were here.
Lie me down again,
unclench my fist.
The plate is white and endless:
they won't arrive;
we won't arrive.

What is this alchemy?
Human time makes no claim
on me today.
Fresh dreams, new stories
oppose our bootless speed.

Unlocking

I like it when the wind subsides
and the grass doesn't move ...
except that you feel a little left behind.

There is the smell of yellowed pages,
fresh bread, old summers, and childhood;
and the mills—their sails turning in the wind,
marking time—and the faded mansions, still beautiful.

Silent memories now, so far back;
it might as well be the beginning.
Memories I can't quite trust,
shifting like clouds, talking over one another,
like wet gravel glinting under the sun.

You see it too; sharing it is the risk of darkening it,
of losing it forever.

Author's Acknowledgements

My thanks to the editors of the following journals and magazines, which have previously published some of the poems contained in this volume, at times in earlier iterations: *3AM Magazine*, *BlazeVOX*, *Eyewear*, *IMPRINT*, *THIS Literary Magazine* and *[PANK] Magazine*. I thank my husband and daughter who have served as motors of inspiration, and Proverse, for their unremitting support.

Advance Responses to *Unlocking*

"Mary-Jane Newton's *Unlocking* is a shape shifter and unpredictable. Each poem gets to you without warning. From ache through sadness to love and resolution, she transforms a kaleidoscope of experiences and emotions into poetry, each poem a small world. Lyrical, funny, aching, brutal, loving, and forgiving, her poetry is as bold as it is gentle."

—**Rose Mary Boehm**, author of two novels and the poetry collection *Tangents*.

"In her second full-length collection of poems, Newton proves that she is a poet on the move. And that move is *forward*. There is a great deal of history in this book— personal and otherwise—but it is all history in the service of *now* and *next*. ... Follow this poet. You'll want to hear what she has to say now and what she'll have to say next."

—**Diane Goettel**, Executive Editor, Black Lawrence Press.

"This is a book of change and turbulence. A book of crisp language and enjambment. A book of voices, from mothers, lovers, Brecht, Vonnegut, Cage, a prison in Sri Lanka, a basement full of poppies, *Is*-ness and the past, which Newton calls "a slippery bed mat" and she asks: Does something that has had all its parts replaced remain the same thing? By the end, *Unlocking* is a book of patience, love and tenderness."
—**Madeleine Marie Slavick**, author of *Fifty Stories Fifty Images.*

"Mary-Jane Newton is a talented poet, and this new collection will hopefully win her new readers. Her style is accessible, playful, and often unsettling—she is unafraid of black humour, the twist in the poem that can surprise a reader who might think these are just poems about motherhood and love. Look again—there is steel and fire here, in powerful, sometimes exotic, poems of war, lust, technology and danger. From her unusual vantage point as a writer of English poetry on the edge of China, Newton is offering a new perspective on 21st century living."

—**Todd Swift**, Teacher in Creative Writing, University of Glasgow, Director and Editor of Eyewear Publishing and Author of "Selected Poems 1983–2013" (Marick Press, USA, forthcoming 2014).

Notes

[1] Tree-dwelling spirit in Japanese folklore.

[2] Then I looked up and found that it had gone.—Bertold Brecht, *Remembering Marie A.* Transl. Dominic Muldowney.

[3] No cat was harmed in writing this poem.

[4] Chinese female name, literally translated, "Pure as snow".

[5] Variety of the common carp. In Asia considered attractive, and often kept for *feng shui* purposes.

[6] Grandmother (Serbian).

[7] German for '*Is*-ness'. A term coined by German philosopher Eckhart von Hochheim, c.1260–c.1327 (also known as Meister Eckhart).

[8] Sargon of Akkad, a Semitic Akkadian emperor who reigned during the last quarter of the third millennium BC.

[9] German sausage.

[10] *Stand Still Like the Hummingbird* is a collection of stories and essays by Henry Miller (published in 1962).

[11] The ship of Theseus (also Theseus' paradox) explores whether an object which has had all its parts replaced, remains fundamentally the same object. It is a philosophical dilemma discussed by Plutarch, Heraclitus, Socrates, and others.

[12] Iceberg B-15 is the world's largest recorded iceberg.